DUNNS' GOOD PUTTING

ORIGINAL GOLF FUNDAMENTALS

MUSSELBURGH, SCOTLAND

Ronald Ross 1858

COPYRIGHT

Ronald Ross 1858 50933 Cologne Germany
ISBN: 978-3-00-065507-4 Cover Design: Ronald Ross 1858
Paperback Edition first published 2020

HOME OF THE ORIGINAL GOLF FUNDAMENTALS

MUSSELBURGH, SCOTLAND

After a ten years' search, and practice, in seeking to cure a slice and wanting to play good golf, it has been determined that the Home of the Original Golf Fundamentals is Musselburgh, Scotland, and that these Original Golf Fundamentals are, still, the essentials of good golf!

The evidence is now before you. Also see our web site, and trust in Henry Cotton too, at:

www.curedmygolfslice.com

As Presented
"To H. H. Ramsay President U.S.G.A. 1932"

PART 2 – GOOD PUTTING

The all-important essentials of good putting are:

1. Proper Line of the Putt & Proper Angle of Clubface Thereto;
2. Touch, or Proper Form of Propelling the Ball;
3. Mind, or Proper Psychological Concentration.

"Reduced to its simplest expression, effective putting depends upon absolutely true hitting, with a reasonable proficiency in distance judging." – ALEX SMITH 1907, OPEN CHAMPION, UNITED STATES AND WESTERN OPEN CHAMPION

CONTENTS

PREFACE

Jack White

THERE seems to be a fairly general opinion that I am a pretty good putter, and I am often asked for hints about this part of the game.

In those days there was a very difficult putting course close to the first tee at North Berwick, and I and the other caddies played rounds for penny sweepstakes on this course while our masters were at lunch. On the whole, I think I drew more than an average share of pennies from the sweeps, and while I always found putting to be a comparatively easy matter - that is to say, as easy as it can be to any golfer - I certainly think that all this practice while I was a very wee boy did me a lot of good.

As I have just said, this putting course was a very difficult one, and it was above all things hard to discover the exact line to the hole. This practice taught me to calculate gradients and their effect on the run of the ball almost instantaneously, so that after a little while I became always very certain of my line, and the rest was easy.

The great thing is to find the line, and my own success with the putter is, as I have already indicated, almost entirely due to my gift for finding the line, and being very sure about it almost at once.

Willie Park finds the line beautifully. Let me say at once that, though he may not know of my obligation, I have one man to thank for winning that Championship, and that I am convinced if he had not been born or had not played at Sandwich the week before the competition, I should not have been Open Champion - that year, at all events.

That man is Mr. W. J. Travis, who won the Amateur Championship in such sensational fashion the previous week.

What impressed me most was not the remarkable putting that he displayed all through the tournament, though it was really very fine, but the simple accuracy and certainty of his long game. He never tried to get any length. He simply tried to place his tee shots at every hole, to make certain of avoiding trouble, and then he depended on his deadly putting to win the hole for him.

And more often than not it did. I said to myself as I watched him, "If this is the class of golf that wins the Amateur Championship, I must try it in the Open," and so I did.

- JACK WHITE, OPEN CHAMPION 1904

INTRODUCTION

Dunns' Good Putting

THIS book is intended as a reminder of the principal points to study in the science of the game. The subject matter of this book is the text by which all instructors taught in the Seymour Dunn Golf School at Lake Placid, N.Y.

"To excel at the game, one should go about it correctly. Since many golfers achieve success with wide varieties of stance, grip, body pivot, etc., it stands to reason that while of very great importance, such matters are not fundamentals of the golf swing.

They are merely matters of style and of method in applying the fundamentals. Fundamentals are basic principles of a theory and these principles should be regarded as inviolable by the student no matter what the expert players may do and get away with.

It is to be regretted that many writers use the term "fundamental" loosely when discussing matters of style, individual mannerisms, or other important, but not fundamental, aspects of golf."

- GOLF FUNDAMENTALS BY SEYMOUR DUNN 1922; STANDARDIZED GOLF INSTRUCTION SEYMOUR DUNN 1934

EPIGRAPH

Henry Cotton & Seymour Dunn

When I studied Bobby Jones's swing I found that his hand action was particularly slack and loose.

Yet, when people asked him about it, he said that there was a buffer action in the swing. This buffer action is what we today call the impact. He was aware that there was a shock at impact. He realized that the ball was 'shocked' off the club and that he had to absorb it.

He wrote about this, but I do not think that many understood what he meant.

I think that what he meant was that he was hitting the ball as though he was driving it under a suspended carpet hanging on a line.

The bottom side of the carpet was the height of his hands; he would hit the ball and the carpet would check his hands, and the club head would spring through below it.

In other words, there was in his swing a sort of left hand against the right, a resistance to the right hand somewhere, and I think people overlooked that, and still do.

Now, when a lot of players today write on the game, they ignore it too. They have been hitting balls for so many years that they do not realize that there is a point in the swing when you have to absorb the shock, to take it in your hands.

Forty years ago Jones saw this and wrote about it, and this also applies to putting. This is worth remembering.

- SIR HENRY COTTON MBE, OPEN CHAMPION (BRITISH OPEN) 1934, 1937 AND 1948; THANKS FOR THE GAME THE BEST OF GOLF WITH HENRY COTTON, SIDGWICK & JACKSON, LONDON, 1980

The majority of players who fail in transmission of power do so because their left hand fails to act as a fulcrum for the right hand to strike against.

The left hand must bear back against the right.

This back pressure of the left hand must be exerted at the moment of impact.

- GOLF FUNDAMENTALS BY SEYMOUR DUNN, OF THE DUNNS OF MUSSELBURGH, SCOTLAND, PUBLISHED 1922

Douglas Rolland "addressing" the ball for full drive
HORACE HUTCHINSON, GOLFING, 1903

CHAPTER 1 - "The Man who can Putt is a Match for Anybody"

As told by Horace G. Hutchinson, 1914

WILLY PARK, always a man of some practical ingenuity, as well as a magnificent golfer, had lately invented and patented a peculiar type of putter.

He had also invented, by way of an advertisement of this crooked-necked club of his, the dictum that "the man who can putt is a match for anybody."

Now Park, besides his other fine qualities, was a very gallant golfer. It had been his way for some years, as soon as some man - be it Douglas Rolland, or any other - had come to the top of the golfing tree, so that everybody was talking about him and saying what a fine fellow he was, to challenge this fine top bird of the roost, and back his challenge with a £50 or £100 stake.

There may have been a tinge of advertisement about it, for Park was a good man of business and the first of the professionals to realize what money there was in establishing golf shops, but chiefly, I think, he played these matches for the pure sport of the thing.

Harry Vardon

So now, Harry Vardon, being beyond dispute, at the tree top, Park must issue a challenge to play him for a money stake, a home and home match, two rounds at North Berwick and two at Ganton.

Now you have to realize that in those days Harry Vardon was so great a man, there was so much keenness to see him play, that when he went out the gallery followed him, they watched his every stroke, and they paid no more attention than if he had no existence at all to the poor wretch who chanced to be partnered with him.

They would trample on this unfortunate creature's ball without the slightest remorse: he was rather lucky if he were not thrown down and trampled to death himself by the throng. Willy Park was a shrewd Scot. He was not going to have any of this nonsense when "the man who could putt" set out to prove, for money, that he was a match for anyone, even for Harry Vardon at his best.

The match opened, therefore, at its very second shot, on the note of comedy. Park had gone a little further off the tee than Harry Vardon, toward the bunker guarding Point Garry Hill. That meant that Harry Vardon had to play first, and after his play of the second shot the gallery made a start to dash in, in their accustomed manner, quite regardless of the other partner to the match.

"Fiery"

Park proceeded to teach them their lesson at the outset. He did not hurry, like a guilty thing, to play his shot, as most of the others who played with Vardon used to do: instead, he left his ball altogether, with "Fiery," his faithful caddie, standing guard over it.

"Fiery" - Willie Park's Caddie

The people crowded forward as far as Fiery, but they were not at all likely to go beyond him, most faithful henchman, and rather truculent watch-dog, with round Scotch bonnet and streamers floating behind, the clubs loose held, out of the bag, beneath his arm - I rather think he would have called it his "oxter" - because he had for years carried clubs before bags came into use, and the fine smoothness and polish of the club handles was apt to be spoilt by dragging them in and out of the bag.

I never heard nor cared what other name he had than Fiery, of which the propriety was written in flaming colours on his face.

So he stood, facing and keeping back the crowd from the ball - a subject not unworthy of an historical picture and by no means to be disregarded as a point in the golfing story of the last fifty years, because he was a type, and nearly the last, of the old Scottish caddies, and because this match was among the last of those of the old style.

Harry Vardon "Will It Go In?"

Park's school was really a generation behind that to which belonged the modern triumvirate.

So Park walked on, having left his ball; he walked on to the foot of Point Garry Hill; then he ascended it, with great leisure, quite regardless that the people raged together, and he looked at the flag, which he did not in the least desire to see.

All he did desire was to teach the gallery their lesson, that he, Park, meant to count for something in this match, that Harry Vardon was not the only player; and when he had thus taught the lesson, which it were better that the people should learn first than last, he came back leisurely to his ball again and played it.

They took their lesson well - a Scottish crowd is not slow at the up-take and has its sense of humour. Moreover, Park was their man, being a Scot. They liked to see him taking himself seriously, and they did not crowd on him inconveniently again. And it was a most amusing match to watch, though just a little pathetic too.

Willy Park was most emphatically "the man who could putt."

He told me that he had been practising putting for that match to the tune of from six to eight hours a day. It sounds terribly dull work; but certainly Park was rewarded for it, for I never saw such putting, day in and day out, as he was doing about the time of that match.

And in the match, he putted extraordinarily. I speak only of the first portion, at North Berwick.

I did not see the latter end of it at Ganton; but I think the result, if there ever could be, from the start, a moment's doubt about it, was virtually all settled on the first thirty-six holes.

HARRY VARDON, By HIMSELF, Stance Putting, 1903

Park putted extraordinarily, but he still had to prove his dictum that the man who could putt was a match for anybody.

Vardon as surely could not putt[1]; but then he played all the rest of the game to a beautiful perfection, whereas poor Park could not drive.

---

[1] Putting does not seem to present any great difficulty to Vardon provided the ball is far enough from the hole to enable him to strike it firmly; it is when the ball is very near to the hole side and he has to strike it gently and, so to speak, try to caress it into the hole, that Harry Vardon's hands and Harry Vardon's putter seem to get at loggerheads, and the result is disastrous, sometimes almost tragic. It is the very short putts which defeat him, and his methods of playing them are rather apt to suggest that the touch in his hands and fingers is not of a sufficiently delicate character to enable him to play these shots which require a very gentle tap with anything approaching confidence. Harry Vardon is a peculiarly pleasing player to watch, none more so in the long game,

He developed, at its worst, that tendency to hook his drives which has always been a danger to him. He arrived on the greens one stroke, or even two, behind Vardon.

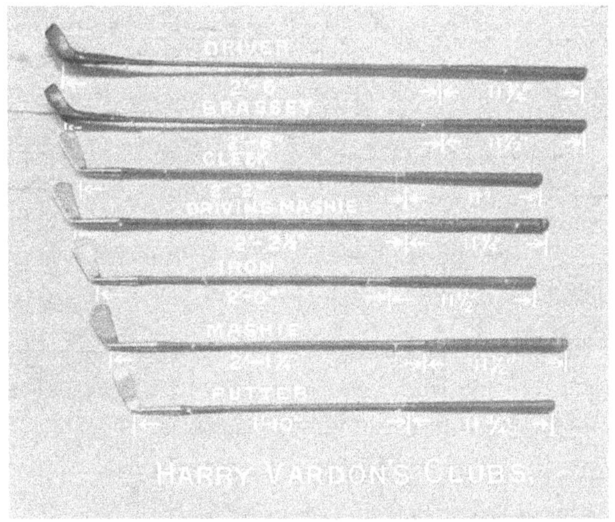

DIMENSIONS OF CLUBS, 1903

But then he put the putt in, whereas Vardon often neglected the simple precaution of laying it dead.

So it went on, Park saving himself again and again by this marvellous putting, and at last, after he had holed one of fifteen yards right across the green, a crusty old Scot in the gallery was heard grumbling to himself in his beard: "The on'y raisonable

---

but the shorter the shot he has to play, the less elegant and pleasing do his methods appear until when he comes to play the most physically delicate of all strokes, viz. the short putt, he cannot by any means be termed an elegant performer. - MODERN GOLF Putting And Putters BY HAROLD H. HILTON, 1913

putt I've seen the day." What he had come out expecting, an all-knowing Providence alone can say.

But the strain of those repeated saves of holes apparently lost was too severe to last. Vardon put a useful balance of holes to his credit even at North Berwick. The final half of the match was to be played on his own course of Ganton. There was only one possible conclusion to it.

At the end of the North Berwick contest I suggested to Park that he would have to re-edit his dictum so that it should run "the man who can putt is a match for anybody - except Harry Vardon," and he confessed, with a melancholy grin, that he believed he would have to accept that emendation.

With the disappearance of the old Scottish caddie, of whom Fiery might very well stand for the prototype, there passed much of the old order of golf, making way for the new.

- HORACE G. HUTCHINSON, 1914

"In putting I have the ball nearer my right foot than the left, with the right elbow slightly resting on right leg. For the long putts, keep the arms clear of knee, as you can't get the same freedom. I always try to putt without spin on the ball. This is practically the only stroke where the wrists work by themselves, without the help of any forearm. I play the ball as if I were playing a push stroke - viz., I strike the ball first, the putter finishing on the ground in the line of putt, after the ball has gone about 3 to 6 inches, which is regulated according to the length of putt." — HARRY VARDON, 1903. OPEN CHAMPION 1896, 1898, 1899, 1903, CHAMPION OF AMERICA, 1900

"Putting has always been a strong part of my game since those days, and I often think that perhaps the training of my eye and the extreme delicacy of touch that came to me through this continual putting with marbles on bricks - I did it for years - helped me greatly when I came to do the comparatively easy putts on real greens." — WILLIE PARK, OPEN CHAMPION 1887, 1889

CHAPTER 2 - "Come on with a Musselburgh Putt"

As told by Robert Ferguson, 1907

I am a Musselburgh man, and, unlike so many professional golfers of the present day, have never been much in residence beyond the limits of my native burgh; in fact, about a fortnight at a time has been the longest period that I have been away from it, except on one occasion.

My birthplace was at Levenhall, less than a hundred yards from the old links, and equally close to "Mrs. Forman's" and the "bonnie wee window," through which refreshment has been supplied to succeeding generations of golfers without the necessity of their breaking the round or leaving the course.

My father was a farm-servant never over-blessed by fortune so that it is not to be wondered at that I should have been early called upon to help to maintain myself.

In those days - by the way, I am now fifty-nine years of age - there was but little choice of employment in Musselburgh.

Papermaking, which is the chief industry of the place nowadays, had not been started in the district, and there was very little coal-mining done either.

Certainly there were the ordinary trades to think about, but a long apprenticeship for little money was not very attractive as a prospect. Naturally, then, living near the links, and knowing that there was a fair chance of making something for the family pot by caddying to the golfers, to the links I turned, and my father did not hinder me.

Musselburgh Links

I confess that the links have always fascinated me, and even in these quieter and harder times the spell has not been broken. I can well remember the pleasure we boys had long ago playing about among the whins, which then grew very thickly on the links, especially at the east end and right up the middle. Much fun we used to get trying to golf with a shinty stick - an Englishman would say a hockey stick - and an old feather ball.

I cannot say that I was ever particularly fond of company, and even when a youngster, used to spend a good deal of the time which I had playing by myself, first with the aforesaid shinty stick, and later with any relic of a club touched up to serve my purpose.

There were more balls lost and found on Musselburgh links then than now, and the boys could always manage to have a few of these in hand, though it was difficult indeed to get a decent club.

We had to put up with any old implement discarded by members of the Honourable Company of Edinburgh Golfers or of the Royal Musselburgh Club, or by old Douglas M' Ewan, clubmaker. I was a pretty big fellow before I could command a club or two of respectable appearance, and I had won my first big event before I had a complete set of clubs of my very own. But of this I will speak later.

I would be not more than eight years of age when I accepted my first engagement on the links, and many a time did I play truant from the old Free Kirk School on likely days to caddie on the links.

My first job was as a forecaddie, and I daresay it would be a couple of years before I was promoted to a carrying caddie. We used to get two shillings per day when acting as forecaddie, with a lunch at Mrs. Forman's consisting of fourpenceworth of bread and cheese.

These were happy days, running as forecaddies to "mark down" the ball as well as to show the line to the hole, for in those days there were no flags in the holes at Musselburgh.

We had to learn to use a few simple signals to make the golfers acquainted with the kind of lie their shot had secured. They were very impatient, those old golfers; and as there was almost always a wager upon the match, you could not let them know too soon what their chances were of winning or losing the hole.

If the ball landed in decent country, the forecaddie had to face about towards the players and stroke his breast downward with his right hand. If the ball fell into whin or bunker, the mishap was telegraphed by a downward stroke of the right fist held out from the body. Two downward strokes conveyed the news that the lie was very bad indeed. A downward stroke and a gentle motion of the hand from right to left indicated that the ball was in the hazard but lying hopefully on a smooth surface.

It was the duty of the forecaddie when a ball fell among whins to mark the place with a piece of paper - which was liftable, of course, by the player - and then hurry on to take up a fresh stand. These little services, which were rendered necessary in the first place by the abundance of hazards, added greatly to the interest of the game.

As in those days the members of the Honourable Company used to come down to Musselburgh and play pretty regularly on the Tuesday, Thursday, and Saturday of each week, there was a fair living to be made on the links for a boy, and I could usually make about ten shillings a week - which for a boy of ten or eleven is not bad.

We sometimes were hard up in the winter time, but the old golfers seemed to be more independent of the weather then, and we often got a job to sweep the snow off the putting greens. Three or four of us would sweep a green when we saw golfers coming out, and then hurry off to the next green, and so on, being paid about two shillings for our work.

When I had reached the age of eleven the links proved a stronger attraction than the school, and I have lived by golf ever since. Early in the morning, and when not engaged by a gentleman golfer, I used to take a round or two on my own account. Very little attention was given to the course. Neither cutting nor rolling was done on the putting greens, and a new hole was usually formed once a week.

Youngsters like myself were not interfered with, except when old John Gourlay, the famous feather-ball maker, who looked after the green, thought that we were playing too long on one putting green.

"Learn young, learn fair," is a true saying, and I set down much of my ability to play the game to the continuous practice I had in those early years, even with wretched clubs.

Jack White, the ex-champion, says that he looks back with satisfaction to a lot of practice he had on a putting course at North Berwick for penny sweepstakes.

Well, we used to have a putting course in front of where the club-houses are now at Musselburgh, and nine holes were laid down in a little space. I never cared much for this putting course, but can remember yet the keen interest I used to take in the matches played on it by gentlemen, often for large sums of money and often by candle-light. I have stayed out late at nights many a time looking on at these queer matches.

For practice, however, I preferred the course proper, then only of eight holes, and I was early a fair hand at approaching, which I consider my strongest point.

With its strong growth of whins and its bunkers, Musselburgh was even a greater test of golf then than now, and I had plenty of opportunity of increasing my ability to steer clear of danger or to play from difficult positions. I believe that this ability to recover made me popular with amateurs, who used to take me as partner in foursomes.

Even as boys we played for small stakes, a penny or twopence, and we used to agree that if one had a feather ball and the other a gutta, the balls must be exchanged after each hole had been played. We knew that the feather ball was a handicap against the gutta, and here I might recall that the gutta was coming into general use when I first began to take an interest in golf; and I can remember one rigidly conservative old golfer, who need not be named - a member of the Honourable Company, now long since passed away - who stuck to the feather ball as long as he could, and only gave it up with reluctance and under compulsion because he could not get any other gentleman to play with him unless he used the newer ball.

I can remember how proud I was when I got my first lot of clubs to carry. They did not make such a great show as a set nowadays. Eight clubs made up a set, and comprised a driver, a long spoon, a middle spoon, a short spoon, a baffy spoon, with its useful sloping-back face, a wooden putter, a track iron, and a cleek.

The track iron took its name from the fact that it was used for getting the ball out of the cartwheel tracks which crossed the links in the line of the now famous, but then unknown, Pandy. It was the forerunner of the niblick. Although heavy irons were a part of nearly every golfer's outfit, gentlemen did not use iron clubs nearly so much as they do now, and the use of a cleek for putting was generally regarded with disfavour.

I preferred to putt with a cleek myself, but have often had to give way to the wish of a gentleman player who had engaged me as partner or opponent, and play with a wooden putter.

Among my very earliest patrons was Mr. James Blackwood, of the well-known Edinburgh publishing firm, and "Fiery" used to carry about the same time for Mr. John Blackwood. These gentlemen were both pawky match players, not very long in the driving, but true in the short game, and very keen. In later years I had the honour of carrying to most of the prominent players who came to Musselburgh.

Lord Shand used to take me out often, and I can vouch that when I was with him he never once was trapped in the bunker near Mrs. Forman's which bears his name. Folk say the bunker got its name because he could never avoid it; I think it might have got his name because he could boast that it had no terrors for him. I have heard him say so.

I was not far advanced in my teens when I played my first match, if these encounters for pennies be left out of account. This match was for a few shillings only, and was against a young fellow named Hood, a joiner by trade, son of the owner of the Royal Oak Tavern. Hood did not care whether he won or not, but I played all I knew, and beat him, though I cannot remember by how many holes.

Just as at the present day, there were a few leading professionals then much in the public eye, notably old Willie Park, old Tom Morris, Andrew Strath, and Davie Park, and these threw the lesser men somewhat in the shade.

The "Musselburgh Putt"

I had plenty of opportunity of seeing and watching and admiring old Willie Park's game. He was a grand player, good all round, but marvellous with his putting.

He used to hole out or lay dead such long shots that the "Musselburgh Putt" passed into a proverb, and even yet old hands are sometimes heard to say, "Come on with a Musselburgh putt," which means to hole out from thirty or even forty yards with a perfectly run ball.

I did not fancy old Willie's iron play, which was a department I had attended to very carefully myself. I think that young Tom was one of the finest all-round golfers it was possible to see playing. Before he came out and won the Championship Belt three times right off the reel and won it for himself, the championship was in the hands of a handful of players.

When I saw old Willie Park beat Tom Morris in one of their big matches at Musselburgh when I was a boy running about the links, I determined to do all I could to come to the front, and was very constant at practice.

Willie Park Jr. at top of swing; full cleek shot

My introduction to the golfing world came when I was eighteen years of age, namely, in 1866, and the occasion was the

Leith tournament, promoted by the Leith Golf Club. £25, divided into five prizes, was offered, and eleven couples were entered, including all the cracks.

Though not particularly fancying my chance, I entered also, and was drawn against a Musselburgh man, Jamie Hutchinson. I played with borrowed clubs, having only one or two of my own, and won the first prize, £10, with a score of 131 for the four rounds of seven holes. Tom Hunter, Musselburgh, was second with 132 (£6). Jamie Anderson, St. Andrews, Bob Andrews, Perth, and old Willie Park, Musselburgh, were also prize-winners. The newspapers made a great fuss about the meeting at the time, the prize-money being considered very handsome.

It was a great day for me. Not only was the money very welcome, but it discovered me to many people who had known me well enough as a caddie simply.

In 1868, "Fiery" and I were sent up to Aberdeen for six weeks, my longest engagement from home, to instruct gentlemen in the game, and it was there that I made my first golf ball, though not my last, for I make and remake them still. In this connection I may mention that a year or two after this I got instruction in the art of clubmaking from old Jack Walker, a clever old club maker, who died practically in harness a year or two ago in London, where he had gone in the service of W. Park & Son. This experience I gradually improved upon, and for half a dozen years in my pre-championship days I had a small club and ball-making business in premises at Links Place, Musselburgh.

But the game was the thing, and I may say I have been matched against most of the front-rank men of my time, and without, of course, boasting - I have to tell what is sober history - I have nearly always finished victorious. Sir Charles Tennant, of the Glen, backed me twice to beat old Tom Morris at

Musselburgh (36 holes), and I was able to do so. My greatest victory over the veteran was at Musselburgh, where I won handsomely in six rounds.

I first secured championship honours at Musselburgh in 1880.

Before that date, despite constant practice, I had never been able to get higher than the fourth place in the great annual contest.

"Constant practice" means much, though hardly so much as what I once did in company with Mr. W. G. Bloxsom, a member of the Honourable Company and many other golf clubs.

We started at six o'clock in the morning one day, and actually played sixteen rounds of Musselburgh Links, or 144 holes!

This kept us going till seven o'clock in the evening, with three-quarters of an hour off for breakfast and the same for dinner. My score was an average of 40 for the nine holes, the highest being 43 and the lowest 36. I beat the amateur, I forget by how many, and won £2,10s.

I retained the championship in 1881 at Prestwick. It was an awful day to golf or be out of doors on, especially in the morning, when wind and rain swept against the competitors.

The effect was to benumb the players. Old Willie Park, who had many droll sayings, summed up the situation. A clergyman asked him how he could play in such weather. Old Willie, unmindful of "the cloth" for a moment, exclaimed in response: "Guid God! When I get ma club up I canna get it doon again."

Weather or not permitting, the championship was mine; and when at St. Andrews the next year I won the championship for the third successive year, my cup was full, and I was very much taken out.

Again, in the following year - namely, in 1883 - at Musselburgh, I tied with Willie Fernie for the championship. We played off, and the Troon man beat me by a stroke rather luckily, for at the 36th and last hole I got down in four, while Willie ran down a long putt with his second.

I have not done a great deal in the way of laying out golf courses, but have planned four or five, besides assisting the late Peter M' Ewan, clubmaker, to layout the Braid Hills course, Edinburgh, which has won a great name for itself.

A teacher of golf - and I have taught thousands - is, like the teacher of anything else, quick to discover the apt pupil. If there is no golf in a person it cannot be driven in. There is no use preaching to some folk. There is no golf in them, and they might as well be told to give it up. I believe that golfing - that is, good golfing - is a gift.

There is one hint that I always give to learners who are putting, and that is to take the line of the putt over a point not more than a foot from the ball. I have seen the line given over a point feet or yards away from the ball and close to the hole. Now the eye - at least, I think so - should command at once not only the ball but the point that is to give the line, and that point, therefore, cannot be yards to the left. This is very natural, but not generally appreciated.

Nerve is practically everything in golf. Certainly without nerve there is nothing to be accomplished. As I say to beginners learning to drive, "Put your shoulders[2] into it," so I say regarding

[2] The upper arm muscles, that is, those about the shoulders swing the arms and the HANDLE end of the club while the muscles of the

the whole game. Nerve, enthusiasm, and practice are the three essentials to success in golf, but to be great in golf requires the gift.

I am not going to say that the younger golfers are better than the old hands. To-day greens are better kept, clubs are better made, and the rubber-cored ball and the perfectly shaped ordinary gutta ball give the player every chance.

Still, it would have been grand to see young Tom Morris and Willie Campbell, my two model players, now passed away, playing under modern conditions against modern "cracks." I don't think there would have been many holes between them.

- ROBERT FERGUSON January 1907

ROBERT FERGUSON 1907
Open Champion, 1880, 1881 and 1882

---

forearms operating the hands through the wrists swing the club HEAD. Standardized Golf Instruction. By Seymour Dunn, 1934

CHAPTER 3 – The Essentials of Good Putting

By Seymour Dunn, of the Dunns of Musselburgh, Scotland

The articles contained herein are the result of the life study handed down by many generations.

"Old" Willie Dunn, the famous Professional Golfer of Musselborough[3], Scotland, who played in the Great Golf Match of 1849, with his brother Jamie Dunn against Allen Robinson and Tom Morris for four hundred pounds sterling a side (on their own green the brothers made a terrible example of the St. Andrews couple, winning by 13 and 12 to play[4]), was the father

---

[3] Musselborough was the original centre of golf, much older than St. Andrews. By Seymour Dunn, 1922

[4] Some Celebrated Golfers by H.S.C. EVERARD, The Badminton Library of Sports And Pastimes, 1890

of the yet more famous Tom Dunn of North Berwick, Scotland, who from the time he was 20 years old till he died at the age of 52 was universally acknowledged the leading authority on golf.

I am the youngest son of Tom Dunn. I was born at North Berwick, Scotland, March 11th, in the year of 1882 and, as my forefathers did, I cut my first teeth on a golf club.

On my mother's side were the Gourlays of Musselborough, and my mother Isabella Gourlay, true to her family traditions, was the greatest woman golfer of her day.

Her father, John Gourlay, was the famous leather and feather golf ball maker.

Gourlay old leather ball

All these family connections have been a great help in preparing me for the great object of my life, which is to get to the very root of this great problem, "The Fundamentals of Golf".

I have not indulged in practicing my own play for the capture of championship honors but have devoted myself to studying the science of the game, and analyzing every detail connected with it.

Hand-hammered gutty

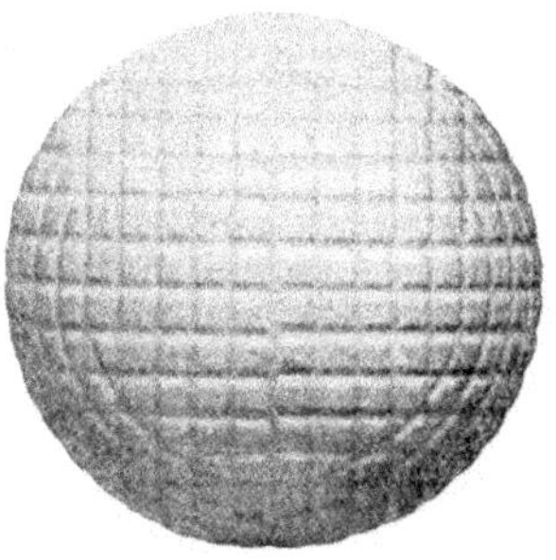

Machine-marked gutty

I chose the work of a teacher as the best field for study for there all manner of questions arise and have to be met with a perfectly clear, correct and understandable explanation.

I originated this code in the year 1897.

This code of golf instruction is complete in every detail and, being elastic, is applicable to all players.

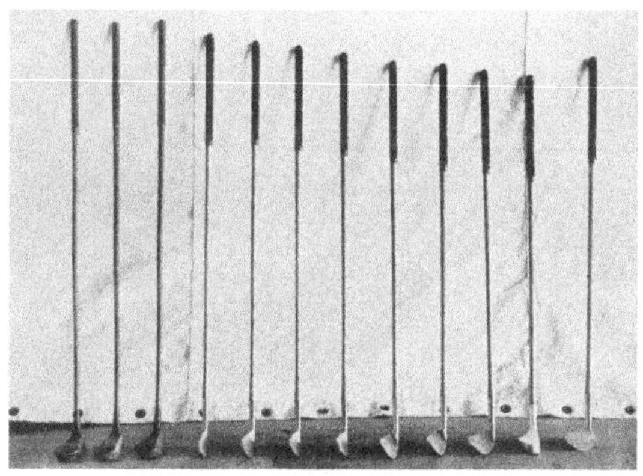

Seymour Dunn's set of golf clubs

Two Ways of Putting

Aside from all matters of style we may say there are two ways of putting:

1) By Mechanical Theory
2) By Intuition

Practically all star players putt by intuition, but all the star players who became famous for their wonderful putting ability developed their putting sense on good sound mechanical theory.

Therefore, I say, learn to putt by aid of mechanical theory so that your stroke will be correct.

When this has become a habit and your ability to putt is developed forget theory and concentrate on the thing to be done, i.e. put the ball into the hole.

Ways to Swing the Putter

There are two entirely different ways to swing the putter:

1) By a Wrist Action Stroke
2) By an Arm Action Stroke

Wrist action strikes the ball a tap, while the arm stroke strikes the ball more of a shove.

I think there is no question that it is easier to gauge the proper strength to send the ball a given distance by the arm shove stroke than by the wrist tap stroke, and certainly it is much easier for the learner.

Sometimes I putt by wrist action, at other times by arm action, depending on how the inspiration leads me.

If I am putting badly one way, I try the other. If that does not work, I change my style of putting. If that fails, I change my club!

In putting the putter head should follow thru; yet I have seen one of our great golfers in a spell of bad putting violate all ethics of putting, to the extent of taking a driver and striking the ball a stabbing blow.

He thereby accomplished some remarkable results. They did not last long, however, and the funniest part of it all was that when he returned to his putter again, the extraordinary act had apparently caused a mental reaction which restored his proper putting touch.

When putting sense and inspiration desert me, I resort to putting by aid of mechanical theory.

Long Putt Stroke

The all-important essentials of good putting are:

1. Proper Line of the Putt & Proper Angle of Clubface Thereto;
2. Touch, or Proper Form of Propelling the Ball;
3. Mind, or Proper Psychological Concentration.

1. Proper Line Of The Putt

On undulating greens, the line to the hole is not always perfectly straight.

A player should make it a habit to walk to a position 10 or 12 feet behind his ball as he walks on to the green to play the putt.

Dip down for an instant and study the putt.

From this low position and with eyes level undulations of the green can be seen that are quite invisible to the player who steps right up to the side of the ball and plays.

Side slopes and little inequalities of the ground are not as plainly discernible as from the low rear view.

SEEING THE LINE OF THE PUTT

The beginner, when asked to do this, may often say: "But this means nothing to me".

Quite so, and it never will mean anything if you do not do it, and learn to see those little things which affect the ball's course enough to make you just miss your putt.

Seeing the line of a putt has for the experienced golfer a meaning entirely different from that which the mere word conveys to the beginner.

An experienced player might look at a putt, and look again and again at it and remark: "I cannot see the line of that putt to save my life". Then all of a sudden he might burst out with, "Ah, I see it now". When he does see it, it becomes as vivid to his eye as tho it were drawn out in whitewash.

The beginner sees the ball and the hole and that's all. He is not able to visualize a vivid picture of the course over which the ball must be sent if it is finally to drop into the hole. That is what we call "seeing the line of the putt". The beginner cannot see the line of a putt because it is a thing which can be learned only by experience.

The point I wish to emphasize is the necessity of learning to see the line of the putt by studying the ground and watching results. The position from which one can properly study the ground and likely line of the putt is illustrated below.

DISTANCE

In the long putt stroke the chief thing is correct distance.

If one takes a special effort to get the strength of the stroke right rather than the line, there will be fewer greens on which 3 putts will be taken than when line is made the chief thing.

On a 30 or 40 foot putt[5] if your ball is anywhere within 2 feet of the proper line and has just the right strength, you may consider yourself dead to the hole, i.e. sure of holing out on the next stroke.

Studying the line of a putt

[5] Come on with a Musselburgh putt. As told by Robert Ferguson, 1907

On the other hand if you make a special effort for line you may find yourself ten feet short or over the hole.

SLOPES

Should the ground slope to the left, the player must play accordingly somewhat to the right of the direct line to the hole, as the ball will always work its way down a slope.

Frequently there is a combination of slopes, one offsetting the other somewhat. A case of this kind calls for very accurate judgment. If the slopes be equal the first slope will affect the ball's course less than the second, because of the difference in the ball's speed.

CLUB FACE SQUARE

When you have decided as to the line, the next thing is to set yourself in position so that you will swing your club in the proper course relative to that line.

Also set the club face so that it faces at a proper angle to it: square. Tho you will find some good players putting off the toe of the putter face, common sense dictates that we should aim to strike with the center of the club face, as it is the only true center of gravity.

2. *Touch*

SWEEPING LIKE BLOW

In the long running up putts, the ball should be struck a sweeping blow, following thru in a straight line, with clubface kept square to intended line of play.

The sweep is made chiefly with the right arm and right wrist.

3. Mind

PROPER CONTROL OF THE PUTTER HEAD

The chief cause of failure to putt well is due to the fact that most players take it too much for granted that just because they have set their putter square and set themselves to swing the putter in a certain line, that they will keep the club face square, and swing it along the proper line.

In 99 cases out of every 100, bad putting is caused by sheer neglect of, or lack of proper automatic control of the putter head.

As they are about to hit the ball they look up as if in anticipation of the ball going astray or the hole running away.

The hole cannot run away and you cannot influence the ball's course with your eye after you have hit it. The mind must not be occupied with the thought, "I wonder if I am going to miss this one".

Because of this thought you look up in a way as if afraid the hole would run away, or as if you could change the ball's course if it did not happen to be right.

Think of the things that will insure your sinking it, i.e. proper control of the putter head, that is what puts the ball in the hole.

THRU THE PERIOD OF LEARNING TO PUTT

While a student of the game is going thru the period of learning to putt, i.e. putting by mechanical theory, a good look should be taken at the ball, then at the hole, and finally at the ball again; thus getting the proper physical and mental "set" for the putt.

The student should not look at the hole or the ball as it travels towards the hole, but keep the mind deeply engrossed on what is being done with the putter head.

This applies to the learner and not to the finished golfer who has already mastered the art of putting.

Fig. 1.- 4. Running up a 40-footer

Fig. 2.

Fig. 3.

Fig. 4.

For the learner it is better to listen for the sound of the ball dropping into the hole than to look up to see it go in.

The student has so much to think of while learning to putt that there will be no thought to spare for anxious anticipation as to the result.

THE PUTTER HEAD

You must remember it is the putter head that puts the ball into the hole, therefore while learning to putt it is the putter head we should watch. I do not mean that you should watch it with your eye, but with your mind.

Think of it and what you are doing with it. Look at your ball, and as you look at it, think of what you are doing with the club head.

Think to keep the club face square and think to swing the club along the line determined on.

AUTOMATIC CONTROL

Just because you have set the club face at the right angle, and determined the proper line along which to swing the club, do not for a single instant think that you have a guarantee that you will keep the club face facing right or that you will swing the club along the line determined upon.

Until you have gained perfect automatic control you must think to swing the club along the line and to keep the club face square.

Fig.1 - 4. Putting By Mechanical Theory

Fig. 2.

Fig. 3.

Fig. 4. Note the eye is still looking at the point where the ball lay, because the mind is still thinking of the control of the putter head.

Short-Putt Stroke

All that has been said concerning the long-putt stroke applies to the short-putt stroke except putting Essential 2) TOUCH, or form of propelling the ball, and special attention to line rather than to the strength of the stroke.

Pushing Like Blow

In playing short putts, do not strike the ball a sweeping stroke, but a distinctly pushing stroke.

Swing the club back the very shortest possible distance that is practical, and carry the stroke thru twice as far forward as you swing it back.

This will materially help you in producing the pushing-like effect in the stroke.

The reason for striking the ball a pushing like blow is that the proper force required to send the ball the desired distance is far more easily controlled.

It is a very common practice to tap the ball in putting, and this very tapping is why a great many players are not able to get the right strength into their putting strokes.

The thing we have to be careful of is the length of the backswing. If the putter head is swung back too far, we get up speed on the putter head too soon and therefore to avoid sending the ball too far we stop the club head at the ball instead of sweeping on thru.

This causes the tap stroke effect.

If the backswing is confined within very short limits you will have to follow thru to get the required distance on the ball and the stroke will take the form of a distinct push.

Practice this pushing thru stroke till it is mastered, then you will seldom ever miss a putt by being short.

Pitching a stymie grip

Short Putts Four Essentials

Should a weakness for missing short putts develop, concentrate on four essential points:

1) Think hard to keep the putter face square to the line to the hole.
2) Think hard to make the putter head swing in an absolutely straight line toward the hole.
3) Be sure to strike the ball a shoving stroke (shove or push it into the hole).
4) Half top the ball or strike it a pulling up stroke, to make it roll.

If you are missing short putts it is because you are failing in some one or more of these four points; don't look anywhere else for your troubles. A change of style might bring about a momentary improvement, but it will not make you a consistently good putter.

In putting, let the right hand be the complete master of the club, and grip firmly with it.

Better still overlap forefinger of the left hand on the little finger of the right hand; this is called "the reverse overlapping grip."

As in the long-putt stroke, learn to play short putts by mechanical theory and in this way develop correct putting habit.

Finally forget theory and place the ball.

In the long-putt stroke special attention should be given to force of stroke rather than line.

In the short-putt stroke special attention should be given to line - force should take proper care of itself.

- SEYMOUR DUNN, LONG PUTT STROKE, SHORT PUTT STROKE, GOLF FUNDAMENTALS ORTHODOXY OF STYLE, 1922, 1930

Fig. 1 - 8. Short putt stroke in motion

Fig. 2.

Fig. 3.

Fig. 4.

Fig. 5.

Fig. 6.

Fig. 7.

Fig. 8.

SEYMOUR DUNN

"Don't forget: Strong hands and wrists are most essential to the golfer. Be sure to develop your hands by regular exercise with a wrist machine." – SEYMOUR DUNN, OF THE DUNNS OF MUSSELBURGH, SCOTLAND, 1897, 1907, 1922, 1930, 1934

"Like most other boys, I had a great chum in those early days, and he was Willie Dunn, who is now in America. He was the son of Willie Dunn, senior, and brother of the late Tom Dunn. We were great friends indeed, and at the same time great rivals in our golf. We were always playing together." — WILLIE PARK, OPEN CHAMPION 1887, 1889

CHAPTER 4 - Dunn was Tutored by Tom Morris

As told by H. S. C. Everard, 1890

TOM, 'old Tom,' is a character, an institution, a subject on which a most interesting monograph might be written.

Wherever golf is played his name is a password; interviewers have interviewed him, journalists made copy out of him; photographers photographed him (including in this latter connexion at least one very skilful lady amateur, who confesses to an absorbing admiration for him); artists have sketched him, with sometimes astonishingly happy results; and, truth to tell, he, as he is known to us now, lends himself somewhat readily to artistic effort - his characteristic attitudes, his hands always in his pockets, except when engaged in the congenial occupation of grasping a club or filling afresh a pipe (which, by the same token, is oddly enough always a bran-new clay for choice), his grey beard, all these and sundry other points go to form an individuality as striking as it is unique.

Allan Robertson and Tom Morris, 1889

It was during Tom's period of service with Allan that their great match was played against the Dunns for *400l.*, indeed this was Tom's first appearance in public in a match of importance, and certainly it was a sufficiently trying ordeal for a youngster to be called upon to go through.

How he acquitted himself, and the result of the match, having been already noticed, need not be here recapitulated.

On the expiration of his time with Allan Robertson, he started business on his own account as club and ball maker, and continued at it for about three years; at the end or which time, about 1851, chiefly through the instrumentality of Colonel Fairlie of Coodham, for whom he had carried clubs, he was appointed custodian of Prestwick Links, just then newly established as a golf course.

In this capacity he remained fourteen years.

During the last four years of this period he was subjected to incessant entreaties to return to his native city: for this length of time he held out, preferring the old twelve-hole course at Prestwick to St. Andrews; but in the end his defences were broken down, and he returned to the old grey city, which he has never since quitted.

On The Links of Musselburgh

Yet nearer to the smoke of Auld Reekie, on the links of Musselburgh, we may see the game received with scarcely less interest by the great mass of the populace.

That was a great occasion there when Bob Fergusson had to do each of the last three holes in three-a-piece to tie for the championship - and did it!

It was growing quite dusk, and from one side to the other the course was lined with a dense mass of spectators, gentlemen of learning, and top-hatted, from Edinburgh, the modern Athens, shoulder to shoulder with grimy miners, who had climbed from the bowels of the earth to see them play.

The Heroes of Their Time

And it is a good links, too, although so narrow, calling out all the best qualities of the golfer. A links, too, which is sanctified by the memory of many a fine match of old days, when Allan Robertson, and the Parks and Dunns of a previous generation, and old Tom Morris were the heroes of their time.

It is there that, besides many other noteworthy clubs, the Honourable Company of Edinburgh Golfers have their clubhouse, and play their 'dinner matches' - matches to which zest is added by stakes large enough to promote interest, yet not large enough to cause ill feeling, wagered over their wine at their dinners in Edinburgh.

And it is a links which is a fine test of golfing prowess - though there be but nine holes. Yet the first three call for long strong driving, following, roughly, the course of the road, which forms the hazard upon the one side, while on the other are bunkers and whins which, alas! are fast going the way of all whins, so that they need the driving to be sure and straight, as well as far.

Then, when we have reached 'Mrs. Forman's,' the third hole, with perhaps a visit to 'Lord Shand's bunker' by the way, we turn to our left, seawards, and leaving the clayey ground of the nature of the first five holes at St. Andrews, we come up along truer links turf, close beside - too close occasionally, if we heel our ball - the sea.

The Brothers William and James Dunn

As will have been already seen in our account of their matches against Allan Robertson and Tom Morris, the brothers

William and James Dunn were in the first rank of players, and on their native green of Musselburgh were well-nigh invincible.

'Dunny', St. Andrews

They were twins, club and ball makers by trade, and remained a long time at home, but subsequently removed to Blackheath.

Willie Dunn in particular was distinguished for a beautiful, easy style, standing straight up to his ball, and was, as we have remarked above, an exceedingly long driver.

In support of this statement, it may be said that he once played a shot from the medal tee on the Hole o' Cross Green at St. Andrews, coming in to the fourth hole, and the ball was found in the little crescent-shaped bunker at the end of the Elysian Fields; this hazard in commemoration of the shot was christened 'Dunny,' a name which it retains to this day.

The distance, as measured on the map, is 250 yards, and although by no means standing as a record for length (indeed the writer has frequently seen longer shots driven), yet it will probably be admitted that anyone who could make such a shot (and in this instance the circumstances of wind and condition of ground were not exceptionally favourable) must be credited with driving powers above the average.

Dunn was Tutored by Tom Morris

After he had been at Blackheath some years, a match was arranged between him and Willie Park, to be played at Prestwick.

Dunn was tutored by Tom Morris, who put him through his facings every day for a week; James Dunn was also a very fine player, though not so long a driver by ten or fifteen yards as his brother; consequently it fell to the latter to uphold the family honour in single matches of importance, whilst the former took his share in foursome play, and could be relied upon as a steady, trustworthy colleague.

He died unmarried; but his brother was married and left a family, one of whom is the popular and highly efficient Tom Dunn, the well-known custodian of North Berwick, formerly green-keeper at Wimbledon. He and his brother Willie maintain the family honour, both being fine players.

The Twa Dunns, Willie and Jamie, Graund Players Baith

This transcript of a conversation held on New Year's Day, 1886, is not only interesting in itself, but contains much sound golfing philosophy. I give it to the reader precisely in the shape in which it has been given to me:

'A gude new year t'ye, Maister Alexander, an' mony o' them! An' it's come weel in, the year has; for it's just a braw day for a mautch. Lod, sir, it aye seems to me the years, as they rise, skelp fester the tane after t'ither; they'll sune be makin' auld men o've a'.

Hoo auld am I, d'ye ask, sir ? Weel I was born June 16, 1821; and ye can calc'late that for yoursel'. Aye! as ye say, sir, born and bred in St. Awndrews, an' a gowffer a' ma days. The vera first time, I think, I hae mind o' mysel' I was toddlin' aboot at the short holes, wi' a putter uneath ma bit oxter.

DUNNS' GOOD PUTTING

Old Tom telling his story

'I was made 'prentice to Allan as a ba'-macker at eighteen, and wrocht wi' him eliven years. We played, Allan and me thegither, some geyan big mautches - ane in parteecler wi' the twa Dunns, Willie and Jamie, graund players baith, nane better - over fower greens.

'An it had na been for gowff, I'm not sure that at this day, sir, I wad hae been a leevin' man. An' noo, sir, to end a long and, maybe, a silly crack - bein' maistly about masel' - ye'll jist come wi' me, an ye'll hae a glass o' gude brandy, and I'll have ma pint o' black strap, an' we'll drink a gude New Year to ane anither, an' the like to a' gude gowffers.'

- H. S. C. EVERARD, ST. ANDREWS, 1890

CHAPTER 5 - Thomas Morris 'Old Tom'

As told by Horace G. Hutchinson 1900

IT is time to close this portrait gallery with the likeness of one of the most remarkable men - best of men and best of golfers - that ever missed a short putt, Mr. Thomas Morris, known to all the golfing world, and to many who are no golfers, as 'Old Tom.'

He has been written of as often as a Prime Minister, he has been photographed as often as a professional beauty, and yet he remains, through all the advertisement, exactly the same, simple and kindly.

TOM MORRIS 'Old Tom' 1907

We may look at this picture of him that shows him at the top of his swing, and may learn from it something of the secret[6] of that golfing skill that put him four times at the head of the list in the play for the open championship - namely, in 1861, 1862, 1864, and 1867; but what no study or that or any other moment of the swing can show us is the virtue by which he has become that which he is - 'Old Tom,' to all the golfing world, of fame to equal Prime Ministers and professional beauties.

The virtue which has given him this position - which he has certainly never sought, and does not seem greatly to value - is, of course, moral and mental, not muscular. It is not to say that if he had not had the physical gifts to make him four times champion, and had he not perpetuated his golfing fame by the unique successes of 'Young Tommy,' his son, these gifts of

[6] The Secret of Good Golf, Standardized Golf Instruction. By Seymour Dunn, 1934

temperament would have been equally conspicuous. They might have remained unobserved by the world, known only to those few who were about him. But his successes in playing the game brought him into a position where they were invaluable and where they were truly valued.

From a 'character sketch' or 'Old Tom's' life, supposed to be from his own mouth, but really the work of that clever writer and good golfer the late Mr. Patrick Alexander, and by him given to Mr. Arthur Balfour for use in the Badminton book on golf, I gather that 'Old Tom' was born at St. Andrews on June 16, 1821.

He was made apprentice to Allan Robertson as a ball-maker, at the age of eighteen, and worked in his shop for eleven years.

The mention of the great name of this worthy, Allan Robertson, at once suggests some reflections and comparisons. It was an article of faith with many old golfers that Allan Robertson was the best player that had ever handled club, and equally, I think, they would have deemed it impious to doubt that he was better than any that ever would handle club in the future. No less than this was their faith in him.

Now Allan Robertson died in 1859. On that doleful day a contemporary wrote: 'They may toll the bells and shut up the shops at St. Andrews, for their greatest is gone.'

If 'Old Tom' came to Allan when he was eighteen and was with him eleven years - that is to say, from 1839 to 1850 - it is an amazing thing that the two should never have had a match together. Yet such seems to have been the case. And 'Old Tom,' most modest of men, has more than hinted to the writer that any reluctance to put their comparative merits to the test was not on his side. It was not that great matches were not the 'mode' - they were eminently the 'mode' in those days that preceded the institution of the championship.

The Brothers Dunn

Thus, in 1843 ('being then twenty-eight years old,' as Mr. Everard says, a chronology that does not agree with that of Mr. Alexander, given above, but is perhaps more trustworthy), Tom was playing a twenty-round match and winning it handsomely against Willie Dunn.

And six years later Tom and Allan played a match on three greens - St. Andrews, Musselburgh, and North Berwick - against the brothers Dunn, and won the match after being four down and eight to play, at which point, we are told, odds of twenty to one on the Dunns were freely offered. The St. Andrews pair thus won the stakes, *400l.,* on the match, as well as the long odds.

These facts are worth noticing, if for nothing else, by way of showing that 'Old Tom' was one of the foremost figures in the golfing world, and constantly playing matches, in the time of Allan Robertson's prime, so that there was no chronological difficulty about their meeting in single contest.

After all, if Allan was loth to put the matter to the issue, we cannot blame him much - should rather applaud him, seeing that he was a professional and not an amateur golfer. For it is evident that he had nothing to gain if he beat Tom.

As it was, the papers said 'their greatest was gone' at his death, and they could not have said more in any case; whereas, had he been beaten by Tom, they might have said a deal less. So at that let us leave it; but the fact remains that if Allan was their greatest, it was a greatness that he had never proved at Tom's expense.

'I left Allan,' says Tom in Mr. Alexander's version of his autobiography, 'to keep the green at Prestwick, and was there fourteen years.'

Then, three years after Allan's death - which would make it 1862 - he came to St. Andrews, and has been there ever since.

During the last years of his time at Prestwick the Open Championship belt was given by the Prestwick Club, and to Prestwick all the best professionals of the day used to go yearly to play for it.

Prestwick from 1860 to 1872 was the single green on which the championship was played.

In the first year of its institution - that is to say, in 1860 - Willie Park won, beating Tom by a single stroke; but Tom was the winner of both the next two years.

Then, in 1863, Park won again, and in 1864 again Tom. In 1865 the winner is a new man, Andrew Strath of St. Andrews. In 1866 Park won his third and last victory, and the following year, for the fourth time, Tom won.

After this for five years (in one of which there was no competition) 'Old Tom's' son, 'Young Tommy,' entered on his wonderful career of victory; and by the time of his sad and premature death 'Old Tom' was truly an old man. Much trouble had been his portion, and new names begin to appear on the championship roll.

And in the meantime, as we have seen, Tom had moved to St. Andrews. His talents had marked him out for the post left vacant by the death of Allan Robertson; and it is in this post that his wonderful qualities have made themselves known and have endeared him to all that have been associated with him.

His unfailing courtesy, kindliness, tact, and perfect temper have kept all the various interests, that are a little apt to run counter to each other at St. Andrews, jogging along without friction.

Town clubs, students' clubs, and Royal and Ancient, all have done, like good boys, what 'Old Tom' has told them to do all these years - has told them with such a way of telling that they had not the least idea they were being ordered about - Tom also not precisely understanding what sort of a tyrant he was; and so they have all gone along together in friendly wise, as if shamed into mutual friendliness by the perfect gentleness of the old man, their common mentor.

Tom can play a good game still. Until six or seven years ago he could be relied on to play a first-class game; and it is only some three years ago that he ceased to take part in the championship play.

As for 'the way it was done,' that may be more or less seen from the portrait. Old man though he is, his swing has not altered much within the writer's remembrance. It is just as it used to be.

He too, like one or two others of the most perfect and most successful golfers that we have referred to, has been guilty all his life of the amiable weakness of missing short putts.

In this connection there is a good old story to be told; but it is so old that, good as it is, I shall forbear to retell it.

'A sound player throughout' is the criticism that one would be inclined to apply regarding Tom's game, as I have known it, in his later years - always with the exception of his unfortunate weakness in the short putt.

There is a great deal of body swing about his driving stroke. It is rather a slow swing, the kind of swing that permits a man to use rather a supple club.

Tom's clubs are supple and flat in the lie, and his swing is a flat one, rather of the 'auld wife cuttin' hay' style, according to Bob Martin's description of his own fine driving manner - generally sending the ball away with a fine flat trajectory that gives it a good run.

It is a style of drive that I should have imagined more suited to the long flats of St. Andrews than to the mountainous Prestwick, for Prestwick was always mountainous, even before the days of its extension.

Nevertheless it was at Prestwick that 'Old Tom' learned a vast deal of his golf, and at Prestwick that he earned his greatest golfing laurels.

Tom Morris at top of swing 1900
Open Champion 1861, 1862, 1864, and 1867

The fine body swing and the fine timing of the moment for letting that swing have its full effect, are the best qualities, as it seems to me, of his style.

He has a fine, half-running, half-lofted, approach stroke with his iron which is very useful, perhaps especially useful for approaching the St. Andrews putting greens, which so often have a low bank before them.

But yet, when all is said, I believe that we must look for the secret[7] of his many and great successes less in any muscular adjustments and methods than in that unruffled serenity of temper that has made him both the man and the golfer that he is.

His figure has a special interest in this picture gallery. Old Tom is perhaps the most remote point to which we can carry back our genealogical inquiries into the golfing style, so that we may virtually accept him as the common golfing ancestor, who has stamped the features of his style most distinctly on his descendants.

'Young Tommy' was his son. It would be singular indeed if so gifted a son had not taken some of his methods from so gifted a father, and on the style of 'Young Tommy' that of the younger generation of St. Andrews players has been more or less consciously modelled.

---

[7] The majority of players who fail in transmission of power do so because their left hand fails to act as a fulcrum for the right hand to strike against. The left hand has to bear back against the right. This back pressure of the left hand must be exerted at the moment of impact if you are to overcome completely the inertia of the ball. ORIGINAL GOLF FUNDAMENTALS. Fundamental 12. Transmission of power. By Seymour Dunn, 1922, 1930, 1934

Thence players have gone out, inspiration has gone out, to all the golfing world in these days of the modern 'boom' in golf, and the ultimate source of the inspiration, so far as we can trace it, is revealed to us in the person of 'Old Tom.'

- HORACE G. HUTCHINSON, 1900

HORACE G. HUTCHINSON 1907

CHAPTER 6 – The Walter J. Travis (WJT) Method

As told by Walter J. Travis 1903, 1907, 1916

About The Value of Putting (1907)

Now I am asked to say something about the principles of golf as I view them, and in particular about the value of putting.

Putting, that is consistently good putting is perhaps the most difficult part of the game, with the possible exception of really first-class approach work.

Driving is largely mechanical, the one essential being to keep fairly straight. In that department of the game you are never troubled about going too far, or if any possible doubt exists on this score you may easily remove it by using a weaker club.

The approach is somewhat more complex, for here accuracy and strength are the elements. Even this part may be largely simplified by using a cleek, iron, mashie, or putter, each having a certain fairly well-defined capacity in respect of distance.

But putting calls for the highest degree of skill and the nicest kind of judgment both as regards accuracy and strength. By accuracy is meant the passage of the ball over an imaginary line between it and the hole. You may possibly be able to keep your ball along this line, but if it is hit too hard it will probably jump the cup, while if necessary strength is lacking it certainly cannot go in.

I am not a believer in long driving, which is not at the same time good driving, and I think that even yet, after the lesson has been many times taught to them, many players hopelessly underestimate the value of reliable putting.

Putting was one of the last matters I made a close study of when I took up the game of golf. The first thing that strikes you when you come to analyse the game is that of the total number of strokes played in a perfect round of golf nearly half the number are absorbed in these little putts on the green.

As I have already said, it took me some time to make this discovery. But when I did I gave my whole mind to a solution of the problem. Supposing a hole has a bogey of five. It is meant that the player shall be on the green in three strokes and shall have two left for the putts. If the hole has a bogey of four, he has to be on the green in two, and has two left for putting. If it is a bogey of three, he must be on the green with his tee shot and has two left for putts.

This is the simple mathematical reckoning of the business; but very few golfers seem to put it to themselves that putting is really half the game; that they have twice as many putts - and, alas! sometimes more - as drives in the course of a round, and that, therefore, bad putting at a hole is twice as costly as bad driving, and excellent putting infinitely more remunerative than the very finest play from the tee. On the green at last, you may, indeed, very often gain a whole stroke; and it is the stroke that tells.

Now watch the man who drives the longest balls all through a round, and count the number of times when, in his desperate efforts to drive farther and farther, he goes clean off the line and into rough grass or other entanglements; then count the number of times that he loses the hole as a consequence of getting into these difficulties, and reckon for yourself how much his long driving has benefited him.

Unless a man can absolutely depend upon himself surely it is better to practise a little self-denial in driving and keep straight. Let your opponent go into the rough grass if he likes. Apart from this view of the matter, consider how very seldom does the long driver, even when his stroke is well played, gain anything substantial over the average driver.

Take a hole of average length - say, 350 yards. The latter drives his tee shot 200 yards, and, being left with a comfortable iron shot to the green, is perfectly satisfied that he has done everything that is humanly possible under the circumstances.

He is nicely in the middle of the course, clear of all hazards, and his second shot will be as easy of accomplishment as it was ever meant to be. He has insured himself against all accidents; that is to say, he has taken twenty or thirty yards off his drive and been guaranteed for safety. Now what does the long driver do? He smites the ball to the utmost extent of his power with the object of outdriving his opponent. Why he does so he himself sometimes does not know.

He cannot possibly reach the green, 350 yards away, in a single stroke.

Walter J. Travis "The most analytical player in America"; Three Times American Amateur Champion and once British
HAROLD H. HILTON, MODERN GOLF, 1913

Therefore he will have to play a second shot to reach it, as his opponent had to do, and the only difference will be that, if his drive has come off as he intended, he may have his to play from a range of 120 yards instead of 150 yards, as in his opponent's case.

That is not a very tangible advantage after all. And he has run all the extra risk of trouble.

If a player stands a chance of gaining a whole stroke by tremendous driving, as distinguished from average driving, at a hole, let him by all means run the sporting risk if so disposed, which he must undoubtedly run when he makes the attempt; but before he makes up his mind to do so let him mentally map out the play at any given hole, and see whether, in the absence of foozles, there is really any good prospect of his gaining that stroke.

If he does this fairly and logically he will see that very seldom will he gain it.

Two Chief Essentials

When I came to study putting at the beginning I realised that there were two chief essentials in it, which once mastered, made it comparatively easy.

The first of these essentials is that the ball shall be made to travel in the proper line for the hole; and the second, that just sufficient strength shall be put into the stroke as to ensure the ball reaching the hole with so very little to spare that there shall be no risk of its running far past.

Anybody can be taught with practice how to putt straight, but nobody can give him a hint of value as to how to putt with the proper strength. This is more an instinct than anything else.

With One Hand Actively at Work

Nearly everybody has his own style of putting, and it is only with hesitation that I advise particular methods; for if a man is a good putter, as putters go, it is probably best for him to keep to the style which he has very likely dropped upon by accident.

Now, in putting, everything depends upon the proper action of the wrists. The body does not enter into the question at all, for whilst a putt is being accomplished it should be absolutely motionless, and when it is not so there is a much greater likelihood than usual of the putt being missed.

I believe that putting should be done always with one hand - with one hand actively at work - that is.

The left hand should be used only for the purpose of swinging the club head backwards preparatory to taking the stroke.

When it has done that its work is done, and the right hand should then be sole master of the situation, the left being merely kept in attachment to it for steadying purposes.

When only one hand is thus employed the gain in accuracy is very great.

Two hands at work on a short putt or a long one tend to distraction.

When the stroke is being made the grip of the right hand should be firm, but not tight, and after the impact the club-head should be allowed to pass clean through with an easy following stroke.

The follow-through should, indeed, be as long as it is possible to make it comfortably, and, with this object in view, at the moment of touching the ball the grip of the fingers of the left hand should be considerably relaxed, so that the right hand may go on doing its work without interruption.

Never hit or jerk the ball, as so many players do. There is nothing that pays so well as the easy follow-through stroke.

And remember, finally, that very best of maxims - "Never up, never in."

Some Chief Principles (1916)

I have found that good putting is largely the offspring of determination, a fixedness of purpose to the exclusion of everything else - concentration, in short. But I rather think determination is the father of concentration, which means the unqualified giving of one's whole mind to the business in hand.

You cannot be dogmatic about putting, as you can about the methods of driving, for there is far more liberty in method.

However, there seems to me to be some chief principles, adherence to which I regard as very helpful.

Stance

The question of stance is a very important one, although in the same day you rarely see two players adopt exactly the same stance in putting. Some of them putt off the right leg and some off the left.

In my opinion, the right leg is the better. It seems a trivial thing but it isn't.

Let there be a preponderance of weight on the heels and the character of the back swing is radically different from that which obtains when the bulk of one's weight is on the balls of the feet.

In the one case the line of retraction of the club is in toward the body, while in the other it is away from it (always supposing, of course, that the right elbow has been gently rested on the hip, of which more anon), so that the ball is struck at different points, totally different results of course ensuing in the direction of the ball.

The Grip

Now, in putting, everything depends upon the proper action of the wrists, and the arms, from the elbows only, more especially the right.

In a longish putt the upper part of the left arm is brought into play, up to the shoulder, but in a restrained way: this in the back stroke.

The body does not enter into the question at all, for whilst a putt is being accomplished it should be absolutely motionless, and when it is not so there is a much greater likelihood than usual of the putt being missed.

Putting off the left leg, 1903

Putting off the right leg, 1903

Putting standing square, 1903

It will be observed from the accompanying illustration that my grip is different from what may be termed the orthodox, the first finger of the left hand overlapping the little finger of the right.

This, I think, facilitates the follow-through and allows a freer relaxation of the grip of the left hand at and following the moment of impact.

Putting grip, 1903

Both thumbs are straight down the shaft and so closely are the hands together that the right thumb overrides the left up to the first joint, so that both hands are working in unison so far as possible.

The shaft is gripped with the fingers, delicately, yet firmly, never tightly. A tight grip, in any circumstances, is fatal to good putting.

The Line

By which, of course, is meant the line to the hole. There are two ways of getting this: first, by sighting, low down, from the ball to the hole, and, second, reversing the process from the hole to the ball. If there be any question, the latter is usually the correct one.

After the line is ascertained, a spot from six to twelve inches should be selected in the shape of a blade of grass or something of the kind, and the putter placed immediately in front of the ball at a perfect right angle to the spot.

Then, without changing the angle of the club-face, rest the club lightly back of the ball, as closely as possible. Too much importance cannot be attached to this matter of getting the line.

After the line is thus secured, the only thing to think about is how hard to strike the ball. In short, you will see, we are trying to make the operation as simple as possible.

After the line is ascertained, and the putter adjusted thereto rectangularly, that part of the business is settled, absolutely.

It is inadvisable to look more than once at the hole after these preliminaries have been arranged, and then only with an eye to the force to be applied. In point of fact, I rarely take a second glance. I have already sized up the situation and usually have a clear idea as to how hard to hit the ball after the first survey. And I find that first impressions are nearly always correct, so that nothing at all is to be gained by more than a single look at the hole.

Really, one has already had two - the first of a comprehensive kind which takes in the distance, the character of the "going," whether fast or slow, the allowance to be made for undulations, or wind; and the second when the question of the line is being determined.

Let there be more and doubt will insidiously creep in. Doubt as to the correctness of one's first conception. Then, by the time this is threshed out satisfactorily - if ever it really is - the line to the hole has been lost. I defy anyone to putt well in such a distracted state. And yet we see the same thing occurring hole after hole, with all sorts of objurgations at the inevitable result.

The Right Elbow

Now we approach, if, indeed, we do not penetrate, the chamber of the mystery of mysteries - the art of putting - the art which conceals the art.

I hold that no man can putt accurately and consistently with a detached right elbow. By detached I mean free from the body. In this way there is no assurance that the line of retraction is identical in any two cases. In all probability it isn't. It could scarcely be otherwise.

But by gently resting the right elbow on the forward part of the right hip and keeping it there until the ball has been struck, the backward and forward swing will be similar every time. That is positive. And results are less apt to vary, always supposing, of course, that the body has remained immovable, which is a prerequisite.

The great merit of this is that one is always making the back swing from a fixed point.

It is like the swing of a gate, or a door. For just as sure as the club-head goes back on a certain line, over and over again, so it will return along the same path, provided of course there is no change of base of the elbow.

It is a perfectly natural movement: there is no straining for effect, no artificial attempt to keep the club head moving continuously along a straight line back of the hole - the prolongation of the line to the hole. That, indeed, is the rock upon which so many players split.

The maintenance of that line (I am speaking now of a straight line back of the ball) necessitates the right arm leaving the side, which, of course, in the absence of any pivotal point, paves the way for mistakes on the return journey.

To convince yourself of the soundness of this, rest your elbow, as you sit, on any part of your right thigh and wave your hand back and forth. It will be found to invariably describe the same arc.

In confirmation of which take a pencil and a sheet of paper, and go through the same performance. Now detach the elbow and see what happens! It will be noticed that the line indicated in the putt proper by the pencil-mark is not absolutely straight. There is a slight curvature to the left. That is as it should be.

Given that the ball is about midway of this line it will go perfectly straight; if to the right or left of the center there will be a corresponding variation.

This central point in the actual putt is of course largely determined by the stance and the position of the hands with reference to the ball. This is a matter which anyone may easily work out to suit himself.

It may be well to add here that the more the hands are ahead of the ball, in the address, the greater the tendency of the ball to go to the right of the hole. Contrariwise, the more they are back of the ball, the greater the tendency of the ball to go to the left of the hole.

In other words, a slice or a pull may be communicated at will, which is well worth remembering.

Going back for a moment to the matter of resting the right elbow on the hip, it should be added that after the ball is struck the right elbow detaches itself from its basic support and follows the club-head along the line to the hole; at the same time the left elbow is allowed to gently rest on the left hip, thus ensuring the follow-through being as straight as possible.

The Short Back

Nearly everyone takes his putter too far away from the ball in the back stroke.

This is a mistake, the shorter the distance, the less chance of any error creeping in. And the shorter the back stroke, the firmer must the ball be struck and the better the follow-through.

Most short putts are missed by not striking the ball firmly, decisively. The holding power of the hole is much underestimated.

By all means putt boldly; the ball will hold the line the better the more firmly it is hit. I don't, by the way, like the term "hit." I should prefer to employ one more expressive, were it not for fear that I might be misunderstood.

The ball is not really "hit" at all; it is stroked, gently coaxed, as it were, into the hole.

Hit, somehow, is associated with a jab, a stab, a convulsive movement - a stop. That may be efficacious at times, but it is not conducive to consistently good putting. Mr. John Low, of St. Andrews, is regarded as a very fine exponent of the art. There is a silky smoothness to his putting.

- WALTER J. TRAVIS 1903, 1907, 1916

"Walter J. Travis, who learned to play golf after he was 35, is probably the most remarkable example of what can be accomplished by constant, patient, untiring practice. No man in America ever worked so hard to become a great golfer as he did, and as reward he has won the amateur championship of the United States three times and the British amateur championship once. Furthermore, he is the only American amateur who ever succeeded in winning the British championship." — JEROME TRAVERS, 1913. AMATEUR CHAMPION OF THE UNITED STATES, 1907, 1908 and 1912

WALTER J. TRAVIS 1903

"He was fifty-three, and some of them were venturing to call him the "Grand Old Man" when he won the Metropolitan Amateur Championship at Apawamis. Percy Pyne, Oswald Kirkby, Percy Platt, Jerome Travers and John Anderson were those who fell by the way as Travis passed along to his victory. He beat them all, and in just the old sweet way he sank a thirty-foot putt on the home green in the final against John Anderson. I think you have heard the names of those people, and know for what they stand. The test in this case was of the most searching American standard; the winner of a national championship is rarely asked to do more for his victory. He won at Apawamis not through skill with his putter alone, but by practically perfect work with all the clubs in his bag and fine steadiness and endurance. That was the marvel of it."

— HENRY LEACH, 1917. THE AMERICAN GOLFER

"Putting should be almost all done with one hand, because, when both hands are used, the one acts against the other; the right hand is the hand which guides the club, and guiding the club is everything in putting, especially in short putts. The right hand should hold more firmly than the left, thus reversing the rule for the grip in other parts of the game. The art of putting lies to a great extent in the player having confidence in himself." — WILLIE PARK, JUN. 1899. CHAMPION GOLFER 1887-89

CHAPTER 7 – Mr. Low A Good Putter

As told by Horace G. Hutchinson, 1900 & George W. Beldam, 1904

In the mind of a good many of us who have watched the course of first-class golf during the last few years, the name of Mr. Low is associated with some very hard treatment.

Luck is supposed to come all even in the long run; but in that case there must be a very good time coming for Mr. Low, to make up to him for past ill-usage.

It is especially in the amateur championship tournaments that he has been so badly treated. Two years in succession have seen him in the semi-final tie, and each of these years he has been beaten, after a halved match, in spite of playing distinctly the better and steadier golf in the extra holes.

Mr F. G. Tait, at top of swing, 1900

In 1897, the semi-finalist that put him out was Mr. Robb - himself afterwards beaten by the late Dr. Allan - and in 1898 Mr. Low was defeated by the amateur champion of that year, Mr. F. G. Tait.

In each case the round of eighteen holes had been halved. In Mr. Tait's case it was only a prodigious recovery at the sixteenth hole at Hoylake that enabled him to get a half of the match; and in both cases Mr. Low had hard lines not to win on the extra holes.

At the twentieth hole he 'had Freddie a regular sitter,' as the situation was commonly expressed by the spectators, for Mr. Tait had to hole a nasty six yard putt to tie; and at the next hole Mr. Tait drove out of bounds, and again it looked any odds on Mr. Low.

But again the former recovered brilliantly, and Mr. Low, playing the hole faultlessly, only halved it. At the next hole Mr. Tait won.

Against Mr. Robb, in the final hole of their match, Mr. Low drove a straight shot, Mr. Robb hit the wall - it was at Muirfield.

Bounding off the wall the latter had a good lie whence he could reach the green, while Mr. Low, in the middle of the course, lay in an iron-skelp, and had to take his iron, with the result of loss of hole and loss of championship.

Of course this matter of Mr. Low's bad luck has an historical and personal interest, but no more; the interest in finding out how he arrived at so honourable a position as semi-finalist two years in succession is more general.

Mr. J. L. Low putting, 1904
Runner-up Amateur Championship 1901

It is a position that he gained by the combination of a variety of good golfing gifts; not the least useful being a light-hearted and brave temperament, that is ignorant of 'funk' or nerves.

On the muscular side there is straightness and fair length of driving and some accurate approach play to Mr. Low's credit, but the factor that is biggest in making the sum of Mr. Low's success is undoubtedly his putting.

He is so good a putter that we cannot, for the moment, name a better, and it is a point especially to be noted that he putts with a wooden putter.

This is a weapon that was universal for the short game twenty years ago. One hardly ever sees the club to-day; we all putt with irons. Perhaps we putt better, perhaps not.

It seems easier to see the correct line off the face of the iron putter; the iron blade seems to give the more definite base line on which to erect our imaginary perpendicular than the wooden putter.

But, for all that, it is a significant fact that some of the very best putters are those who stick to the old wooden weapons.

About the value of the wooden putter for running a long putt up to the hole there can be no doubt; we can all do that part of the business better with wood than with iron. But it is the short putts that bother most of us when we take the wood to them.

They do not bother Mr. Low, however, nor several of those very excellent putters that putt with the wood; and if Mr. Low continues putting, and putting so well, with his wooden putter, it is more than likely that he will produce a reaction, and that we shall see the wooden putter winning its way into favour again.

Mr. J. L. Low approach putt, 1904

In the meantime there are also very many men - the amateur champion, Mr. F. G. Tait, notably - who are uncommonly good with the iron putter; so perhaps there is more in the method than in the instrument.

A Very Free Blow

And in the method as exhibited by Mr. Low there is something very noteworthy, and the more noteworthy because it is exhibited by other fine putters with the wooden instrument also, and this is that they all seem to draw the club very far back away from the ball before striking, and to strike the ball a very free blow.

Another very good putter indeed, though he is not a first-class player, who has this peculiarity is Mr. Linskill, who did so very much to help the Cambridge University Golf Club in the days of its infancy.

A third was Jamie Allan, who in his best day was as fine a player with all his clubs as ever played golf.

All these seemed to use the wrists a great deal in the stroke with the wooden putter.

In Mr. Low's putts, the ball seems to be hit so hard and freely that it must inevitably go far beyond the hole, but though he is as bold a putter as he is accurate, and always gives the ball a chance, he seldom runs it out of holing; indeed, no man is better at that important detail of the game - laying the long putt dead.

There is a very good point about Mr. Low's putting - that he does not dwell very long on his aim. He does not get 'broody' over his putts. He studies the putt well from behind the ball, and when he has satisfied himself of the proper line from ball to hole he goes up to his putt, takes a final glance at the hole, lays the putter to the ball and putts quickly - and with deadly effect.

Mr. J. L. Low putting, 1900

Perhaps this quickness is part of the secret of his success, but I expect that his good nerve and good eye have more to do with it. At the same time, if a man be inclined to be nervous, there is no doubt that a continued dwelling over the putt gives time and opportunity for all the demons of doubt and irresolution to assail his soul - a review of the dreadful consequences of the prospective miss looms large between his eye and the ball, and obscures the clear view that the one should take of the other; and the shorter the time that can be given for these nightmares to take shape the better.

Therefore we believe that there is wisdom in Mr. Low's method, a wisdom that is fully justified of all the progeny of well-played putts that she produces.

It is not while we are studying the line from ball to hole, or again from hole to ball - as Park so wishes us to do - that these ghosts throng in upon us to frighten us. All that is good business.

We are wishing all the time to find out the lie of the ground and the line of the putt - there is then no space in our fully occupied minds for the ghosts to slip in. But it is after we have begun to address ourselves to the ball and are standing over it that we begin to think of all manner of things in heaven and earth.

Why we sometimes delay so long before striking we should often be puzzled to say.

It is not that we are reconsidering the line, or the strength, or are occupied in any useful calculation. Rather it seems to be that we have fallen into the habit of thinking that a decent interval must elapse between our address to the ball and our striking of it - that it is, as it were, disrespectful to the putt to play it without standing in the attitude of address for the canonical length of time.

We cannot say why we delay so long; but the effect, no doubt, is to make us miss many an easy putt. The only consolation is in the reflection that it has probably caused our opponents, in their natural exasperation at our delays, to miss quite as many; but Mr. Low's speedier methods are the better ones, both for oneself and partner.

- HORACE G. HUTCHINSON, 1900

"Look over the line of putt, decide how keen or how slow the green is, and then decide definitely just how hard and on just what line you must hit the ball. On taking your stance, putt with the ball about opposite your left ankle with about two-thirds of your weight on the left foot. Give your right hand about two-thirds control with the left largely used to steady the club and help hold it on the line. Keep a firm grip never a tight one." — WALTER HAGEN, APRIL 1926. OPEN CHAMPION, GREAT BRITAIN, P.G.A., 1924

CONCLUSION

"Learn To Use The Hands Properly"

Experience has taught me that the primordial thing is to teach a pupil to find the ball, without any specific swing action.

Once he can make a contact he can work on a method, hoping that the method will make the contact more mechanical.

Sixty years ago I remember that outstanding instructor Seymour Dunn proclaiming that golf was 85 per cent hands and only 15 per cent body.

Nothing in a lifetime's experience in golf has happened to make me think otherwise. How right he has been!

Many of the old champions stressed that 'when your legs go, you are through winning'; Sam Snead during his 1979 trip to

Australia announced that he was almost through with competing in the 'Big leagues' for his legs had gone, and of course strong legs are essential for control.

Accept this as a fact: learn to use the hands properly, and like me you will enjoy a lifetime of pleasure-golf.

- SIR HENRY COTTON MBE, OPEN CHAMPION (BRITISH OPEN) 1934, 1937 AND 1948; THANKS FOR THE GAME THE BEST OF GOLF WITH HENRY COTTON, SIDGWICK & JACKSON, LONDON, 1980

“

”Well, I’m not too good,” I said. “My putting is shot to

pieces, and unless it gets together again I’m just going to have to quit the tour. I was hoping that you might be able to help me.” “Absolutely,” he said. “You come right on over. I’m sure all you’ve lost is your confidence, but you come over and we’ll get that confidence back again for you and get you back to a good putting stroke.” I drove over to Horton’s club and for an hour we practiced on the putting green. He talked to me about what a putting stroke should be and what I could do about smoothing mine. I could feel the confidence ebbing back into me as he talked. Horton explained that putting was almost entirely a right-handed stroke and that the left hand was there only to help keep the blade on line. My stroke came back. It was a miracle. Horton couldn’t have been more considerate and I can never thank him enough for what he did.” — TONY LEMA, 1964. (BRITISH OPEN CHAMPION)

Also available in this series:

DUNNS' FIVE LESSONS

Part 1: Learn of the Five Mechanical Laws of the Golf Swing - Fundamentals 1 to 5 - to become consistently accurate

ISBN: 978-3-00-059837-1 Published 2018

www.originalgolffundamentalsdunns5lessons.com

DUNNS' GOOD PUTTING

www.ingramcontent.com/pod-product-compliance
Ingram Content Group UK Ltd.
Pitfield, Milton Keynes, MK11 3LW, UK
UKHW022012260726
13994UKWH00006B/2435

9 783000 655074